A Gift For:

Ms. Bindu Roberts

From:

Anthony Cox

* * *

Apples and Chalkdust

for Teachers

by

Vicki Caruana

BOK5060

GIFT BOOKS
from Hallmark

HONOR
BOOKS

This edition published in 2001 by Honor Books
exclusively for Hallmark Cards, Inc.

www.hallmark.com

Copyright © 2000 by Vicki Caruana

All quotes without attribution are the original works of the author
and compiler.

Introduction

September begins with a bang! You're bursting with energy, ready to try a dozen new strategies and fresh ideas. But by December you're running low in patience and budget money. The slump of discouragement settles in.

Amid the flurry of chalkdust and marked papers, these fun quotes and original bits of wisdom by a veteran educator are glowing with practical inspiration to help you renew your perspective.

As you reflect on your calling and balance your outlook, you'll be encouraged to meet the special challenges and concerns teachers uniquely face each day.

On days when you wonder why you ever became a teacher, pick up this little treasure and recapture the moment that inspired you long ago. It will carry you the whole year through!

*To furnish the means of
acquiring knowledge is . . .
the greatest benefit that can
be conferred upon mankind.*

A teacher affects eternity;
he can never tell where
his influence stops.

—HENRY ADAMS

❊ ❊ ❊

*Your successes may not show up
in the classroom. Sometimes they
show up when you expect them the
least and need them the most.*

Encouragement is
oxygen to the soul.

—GEORGE M. ADAMS

9

Change your thoughts and
you change your world.

—NORMAN VINCENT PEALE

✳ ✳ ✳

*On days when you wonder
why you ever became a teacher,
close your eyes and recapture
the moment that inspired
you long ago.*

Experience is not what
happens to a man. It is
what a man does with
what happens to him.

—ALDOUS HUXLEY

The ultimate measure of a man is
not where he stands in moments
of comfort and convenience,
but where he stands at times
of challenge and controversy.

—MARTIN LUTHER KING JR.

✳ ✳ ✳

*Try to turn every situation,
positive or negative, into
a learning experience.*

Our task . . . is not to
fix the blame for the past,
but to fix the course
for the future.

—JOHN F. KENNEDY

Failure is only the
opportunity to begin
again more intelligently.

—HENRY FORD

✳ ✳ ✳

*If a great many of your
students fail at some task,
leave your pride at the door and
look to yourself for solutions.*

44

Never, never, never,
never, give up.

—WINSTON CHURCHILL

Do what you can, with
what you have, where you are.

—THEODORE "TEDDY" ROOSEVELT

✳ ✳ ✳

*You may not always be
given adequate time to meet
the expectations required of you.
Work heartily. Stay focused
on the task instead of the
inconvenience it presents.*

16

By learning you will teach;
by teaching you will learn.

—LATIN PROVERB

The quality of a person's life is
in direct proportion to their
commitment to excellence.

—VINCE LOMBARDI

✳ ✳ ✳

*Take time to look at the
winning team and find
out what they do to win.*

If a child lives with praise,
he learns to appreciate.

—DOROTHY NOLTE

One mother teaches more
than a hundred teachers.

—JEWISH PROVERB

* * *

Be grateful for parents who
involve themselves in their
child's education. They can
make your job so much easier.

Motivation is when
your dreams put
on work clothes.

—PARKES ROBINSON

If you judge people,
you have no time to love them.

—MOTHER TERESA

* * *

If you miss the little things,
you miss the vast majority of life.

See everything;
overlook a great deal;
correct a little.

—POPE JOHN XXIII

If there be any truer measure
of a man than by what he does,
it must be by what he gives.

—ROBERT SOUTH

* * *

*If you're a seasoned teacher,
take steps to make new
teachers feel welcome.*

Look to the experience of others
who have gone before you.

They are there to offer comfort
as well as guidance.

Nothing in the world can
take the place of persistence.

—CALVIN COOLIDGE

✳ ✳ ✳

If you give up,
you give up on your students.
They deserve your perseverance.

Little by little does the trick.

—ABRAHAM LINCOLN

Be sure you put your feet in
the right place, then stand firm.

—ABRAHAM LINCOLN

* * *

*There will be times when
you must stand on principle,
even when it is unpopular.*

In the arsenal of truth,
there is no greater
weapon than fact.

—LYNDON B. JOHNSON

Education is not the filling of
a pail, but the lighting of a fire.

— WILLIAM BUTLER YEATS

* * *

*The fire you light in your
students for learning will
affect them for a lifetime.*

*Provide the gift of understanding
and encouragement.*

*You never know what gifts
you'll allow to emerge!*

I can live for two months
on a good compliment.

—MARK TWAIN

❋ ❋ ❋

*Invest in your students, show
your belief in them, compliment
them, and acknowledge their gifts.*

32

An idea is salvation
by imagination.

—FRANK LLOYD WRIGHT

It takes time to save time.

—JOE TAYLOR

* * *

*Show your students that
they matter to you.
Come to class prepared!*

Leave as little to
chance as possible.
Preparation is the
key to success.

—PAUL BROWN

You've got to continue to grow
or you're just like last night's
cornbread—stale and dry.

—LORETTA LYNN

* * *

Spice up your teaching.
Bring a new excitement
into your classroom.

Transform futures with
adventure and creativity!

Kindness is a language
which the deaf can hear
and the blind can see.

—MARK TWAIN

✳ ✳ ✳

*Next time you feel
nervous, tired, or stressed,
indulge in a good laugh.*

*Your smile could be
just what your students
need today.*

He who conquers others is strong. He who conquers himself is mighty.

—H. L. MENCKEN

* * *

Allow your opinions to be enriched by the insight of others.

*Make understanding
your priority before
trying to be understood.*

It is sheer waste of time
to imagine what I would
do if things were different.
They are not different.

—DR. FRANK CRANE

* * *

Things can be different only if you
can make them different.

Make sure you choose your
own path and stick to it.

Don't find fault. Find a remedy.

—HENRY FORD

✳ ✳ ✳

*Be gracious and understanding
in dealing with parents, keeping in
mind that they are entrusting you
with their most treasured gifts.*

Learn to diffuse frustrations
by placing your energies
into seeking positive,
active solutions.

The heart benevolent and
kind . . . most resembles God.

—ROBERT BURNS

* * *

*A heart of compassion and belief
can be the very thing which
causes a student to "make it."*

Treat people as if they were
what they ought to be
and you help them to become
what they are capable of being.

—JOHANN WOLFGANG VON GOETHE

When you make a mistake,
admit it; learn from it
and don't repeat it.

—BEAR BRYANT

* * *

Self-reflection clarifies
better than any mirror.

The highest reward for
a man's toil is not
what he gets for it,
but what he becomes by it.

—JOHN RUSKIN

A good deed is never lost;
he who sows courtesy
reaps friendship, and he who
plants kindness gathers love.

—SAINT BASIL

✳ ✳ ✳

*Be an advocate for
someone who really needs it.*

No act of kindness,
no matter how small,
is ever wasted.

—AESOP

Between whom there is
hearty truth, there is love.

—HENRY DAVID THOREAU

* * *

*If your motive is really to help,
you'll find a way to
speak the truth in love.*

52

Tell parents the positive first.
It makes the negative
more palatable later.

If a friend is in trouble,
don't annoy him by asking him
if there's anything you can do.
Think of something
appropriate, and do it.

—E. W. HOWE

✳ ✳ ✳

*Never use words when
action is required.*

No one is useless in the world
who lightens the burden
of it for anyone else.

—CHARLES DICKENS

The man who is born with
a talent which he is meant
to use finds his greatest
happiness in using it.

*When you do what you love,
you do it well, no matter
the circumstances.*

56

The secret of success is
constancy to purpose.

—BENJAMIN DISRAELI

The good life, as I conceive it,
is a happy life. I do not mean
that if you are good you will
be happy—I mean that if you
are happy you will be good.

—BERTRAND RUSSELL

* * *

*Give your students a chance, and
they might well make you proud.*

Nothing has a better effect
upon children than praise.

—SIR PHILIP SIDNEY

Be a friend to thyself,
and others will be so, too.

—THOMAS FULLER

✳ ✳ ✳

*Reach out and get to know
your colleagues. You may
discover a kindred spirit.*

*Is there a teacher on your staff
who could benefit from your
encouragement today?*

Shoot for the moon.
Even if you miss it you
will land among the stars.

—LES (LESTER LOUIS) BROWN

* * *

*Never underestimate
the power of expectation.*

62

There are only
two lasting bequests we
can hope to give our children.

One of these is roots;
the other, wings.

—HODDING CARTER

A good laugh is
sunshine in a house.

—WILLIAM MAKEPEACE THACKERAY

* * *

*Let your students see you laugh,
and you let them see your heart.*

*Remember not to get
so wrapped up in life
that you miss the beauty
that is around you.*

My business is not to remake
myself, but [to] make
the absolute best of
what God made.

—ROBERT BROWNING

* * *

*Daily make an effort to
grow and become your best.*

There's only one corner of
the universe you can be
certain of improving and
that's your own self.

—ALDOUS HUXLEY

Take the attitude of a student.
Never be too big to ask
questions. Never know too
much to learn something new.

—OG MANDINO

✳ ✳ ✳

Find someone who is doing
what you want to be doing well,
and ask him or her how it's done.

I make progress by having
people around me
who are smarter than I am—
and listening to them.

—HARRY J. KAISER

Imagination is more
important than knowledge.

—ALBERT EINSTEIN

✳ ✳ ✳

*Is your classroom
a safe place to dream?*

Dare to be different!

*Allow individuality
in your students.*

*Only then will they
discover their true potential.*

Until you try, you don't
know what you can't do.

—HENRY JAMES

* * *

*Some of the best discoveries
are made when we simply try.*

*Quality schools are
the result of quality teachers
going above and beyond
the call of duty.*

Education is helping the child
realize his potentialities.

—ERICH FROMM

✳ ✳ ✳

*Choose not to label your students
by their behaviors. Help them
evolve into something better
than they thought they could be.*

*Your undying commitment
may well be met by
undying gratitude.*

It is impossible for a man to
be made happy by putting
him in a happy place, unless
he be first in a happy state.

—BENJAMIN WHICHCOTE

* * *

*Attitude is everything! If you
are unhappy with where God has
placed you, look inside your heart.*

Though we travel the world
over to find the beautiful,
we must carry it with us
or we find it not.

—RALPH WALDO EMERSON

You cannot shake hands
with a clenched fist.

—INDIRA GANDHI

* * *

Don't panic when adversity comes.
Embrace it and give it the
chance to help you grow.

One of the best ways
to persuade others is
with your ears.

—DEAN RUSK

There is a great man, who
makes very many feel small.
But the real great man
is the man who makes
every man feel great.

—G. K. CHESTERTON

✳ ✳ ✳

If you find yourself frustrated
with others because they are
failing to meet your expectations,
check your own standing first.

Give to every other
human being every right
that you claim for yourself.

—ROBERT G. INGERSOLL

A place for everything,
and everything in its place.

—SAMUEL SMILES

* * *

Need help getting organized?
Find someone whose classroom
you admire and ask for help.

*Organization brings peace
and makes room for creativity.*

Persistence propels
potential to perfection.

— SOICHIRO HONDA

✳ ✳ ✳

*Begin the positive cycle of
achievement. Stretch your students
with a heart of enthusiasm.
Help them experience the
thrill of accomplishment!*

Accomplishment
influences confidence,
and confidence influences
accomplishment.

—HAROLD S. HOOK

Act enthusiastic and
you become enthusiastic.

—DALE CARNEGIE

✳ ✳ ✳

*The way you travel through life
is the most powerful legacy
you can give your students.*

The real secret of
success is enthusiasm.
Yes, more than enthusiasm,
I say excitement.
I like to see men get excited.
When they get excited they
make a success of their lives.

—WALTER P. CHRYSLER

Statistics are no
substitute for judgment.

—HENRY CLAY

✳ ✳ ✳

*Remember that teaching
is more than high test scores;
it is also enriching lives.*

*Every once in a
while ask yourself,
Am I on track?*

It is not what a man does
that determines whether his
work is sacred or secular.
It is why he does it.

—A. W. TOZER

* * *

*On days when you wonder
why you ever became a teacher,
recapture the moment that
inspired you long ago.*

Love what you are
doing and show it!

−HELEN BOEHM

Every child is an artist.
The problem is how to remain
an artist once he grows up.

—PABLO PICASSO

❋ ❋ ❋

*Encourage the artistic soul
discovered in your students.*

We cannot form our
children as we would wish;
as God has given us them.
So we must accept and love,
educate them as we best may,
and rest content.
For each has different gifts;
every one is useful, but
in its proper way.

—JOHANN WOLFGANG VON GOETHE

About the Author

A veteran educator and curriculum designer, Vicki Caruana loves to encourage teachers! She is frequently a featured speaker at conferences for educators, home-schoolers, and parents. Currently she spends most of her time writing for a wide variety of publications, including *ParentLife* and *Parenting for High Potential.*

She credits her inspiration to her first grade teacher, Mrs. Robinson at Mount Vernon Elementary School, who influenced her decision at age six to become a teacher, and to her family with whom she now lives in Colorado Springs, Colorado.

For additional information on seminars, consulting services, scheduling speaking engagements, or to write the author, please address your correspondence to:

vcaruana@aol.com